$3.50

THE ISLE OF THE LITTLE GOD

POEMS 1964–1980

THE ISLE OF THE LITTLE GOD

POEMS 1964–1980

MARY FERRARI

THE KULCHUR FOUNDATION

Some of these poems have appeared in *Adventures in Poetry, Angel Hair, Another World, Attaboy, The Boston Phoenix, Broadway: A Poets' and Painters' Anthology, Choice, Equal Time, Extensions, Glassworks, The New York Quarterly, Rocky Ledge, Un Poco Loco, Women/Poems,* and *The World;* and in two earlier collections: *The Flying Glove* (Adventures in Poetry, 1973), and *The Mockingbird and Other Poems* (Swollen Magpie, 1980).

THE ISLE OF THE LITTLE GOD
by Mary Ferrari

FRONT & BACK COVERS
by Jennifer Bartlett

Published by The Kulchur Foundation
888 Park Ave., N.Y., N.Y. 10021
Copyright © 1981 by Mary Ferrari

Library of Congress Cataloging in Publication Data
I. Title.
PS3556.E7253I8   811'.54   81–2163

ISBN-0-936538-02-3
Printed in the U.S.A. by Capital City Press, Inc.
Montpelier, Vermont

for Frank, Paul, Mary Anne, John and Jim

CONTENTS

1964–1969

THE SEINE

Someday I shall marry perhaps
and go by ship to France to live
stopping first in Rome to see
the Pope and the Pincio Gardens. . .

You will find Paris a gray city
with none of New Orleans' color.
A disappointment at first
until you know the bridges
and Saint Julien le Pauvre
crumbling and small, hiding behind
a broken tree across the Seine
from Notre Dame
(the contrast there is strong).
You will discover
that what Apollinaire
said about the Seine is true.

This dream of yours—what can it mean?
Surely you are who you are. I understand
that you are married and at first
spent four years in France.
I can't be wrong!
You have known all this before.
Yes! But without knowing
what it means.
Yet everything remains.
I can still hear the bellowing music
of our last landlady, Madame Troisier's voice
as she shouted for her daughters,
her servants, my husband or for me.   Franck,
mon chèr Franck, dîtes-moi,

qu'est ce qu'il se passe au Maroc?
An aging semi-invalid
she lay among her pillows reading
Camus and Gide.
Solange, her obstetrician daughter,
ran to her sports car,
shouting back, Je déjeune chez Annette!
(Her lawyer sister.)
Madame Troisier's servants
were good women who constantly complained:
Elle est méchante!
très égoiste!
Our babies slept and lisped
their French beneath rose trees
in the stone walled garden.
Their brusque and single nurse,
Marie-Alberte, roared at me one day:
Je suis très féminine, moi, très
féminine! I didn't know what to say.
Another day she spoke the truth:
Je suis très bien chez les enfants
mais pas chez les adultes.
Her parents died when she was young.
La joie venait
toujours après la peine.
I remembered the shattered smile of the poor woman
who came daily to collect my garbage
for her potage
and a bridegroom bringing Beaujolais
and bread. I'm twenty-nine
on rue Jouvenet my sweater's pink at three o'clock
gold shadows run across the room
the room moves I stand still
I hear a baby crying in one more hour the mail
will be here will Frank be home
at seven or eight
have I a book to read I've finished
Orwell's *1984* I wish that I could write!

Our furniture was ugly
because Madame Troisier
was an intellectual, her son-in-law
said. Our first patron
Madame Delacroix-Froust
had ant eyes and a pruney mouth.
She seemed always to be waiting
for the smell of burning beets
to emanate from our room.
It was full
of good imitation Henry II
said an American visitor
who had lived in France for
years. We had a little hot water
every other day and two burners to cook
on in the salle des bains
where my husband's socks
hung drying around the bidet.

I was pregnant in our second
summer. My husband
went out each morning to buy a carafe
of lukewarm milk.
I drank it for the baby's bones
in Paris and Berlin.
In East Berlin I photographed red geraniums
on a ledge where a window used to be
until Immanuel and Frank came running
down from Stalinallee
shouting, The Police!
In West Berlin in '56
I read Stevenson's speeches
in the Paris Trib at Kurfurstendam sidewalk
cafés while drinking coke
to keep from being ill. Later on, in winter
I read *War and Peace* at Vence and when
I got to Lisa's death in childbirth my own
fears rose and stayed high.

My husband went to India
and I to New York.
I sank into my parents' sofa.
Long Island was as flat as ever
but for once I was contented
to be there.

Your wife is a good worker
the Pakistani said
as I passed the canapés and tea.
A Hindu spent his first
Paris night in our apartment, denounced
America but said that my husband
and I were Indians at heart.
A French friend introduced me
as an American girl typique.
My husband was becoming Africa's great
friend. My college friends had been
conventional. I was the only dreamer
in the group, yet knowing them well, each
was unique. I missed their
company. A Scottish journalist
gave us Belloc's books
and went with us to Saint Sévérin
where we sang: Le Seigneur est
mon berger. A good show
was what he said. Père Plé
arrived as the clock struck seven
in mud-spotted white wool.
He loved good food and wine,
Paris and Bach.

I gave spiritual self-advice I couldn't keep.
Unless the grain of wheat
falls into the ground and dies. . .   In Teilhard
de Chardin I later read
becoming must come first or else you cannot die
in order to bear fruit.

An Irishman came for dinner and said,
American women are the worst
and "God bless you" when he left.
Our second child was born in Paris.
The delivery room was small and green.
Elle est trés sensible, the nurse said
when I cried for something to kill the pain.
Anyway, I saw the blood-stained
baby girl as soon as she was born
and so did Frank. We drove home
through the Bois de Boulogne.
Another May when I was four
my father and I brought home my mother
and my sister Anne just born.

Sunday afternoon, half-eaten birthday cake
is on the table. River shadows run·
across the bed until the afternoon
is spent. Gay Berlioz and red and yellow
winter tulips are floating in my mind.
Marriage is lonelier than I had
thought but what I'd thought was an
abstraction. God is wonderful
hope persistent as the Seine, and a forestful
of birds in Bach's Fourth
Brandenburg Concerto are delirious
with joy.

Hand in hand we walked through
Paris nights. Above our heads, the lamplight
through a green riverbed of leaves
was sweet as stars. La joie venait
toujours après la peine. I've put
the beginning at the end.

ETERNITY

> *for Kenneth Koch*

at the end of every cigarette that burns there is of course
a soft little bright light which means
hope! eternity! so you are not
killing yourself when you
smoke you are preparing for
heaven where the loving lavender
cigarette angels have soft ash wings
or for hell where a flaming cigarette forest makes
a marvelous explosion in which
at last you are involved

Today I go to school
to study the romantic poets.
Sylvia from Trinidad and now
the Bronx is coming to take care
of the children. Now I am on the train
trying to read Wordsworth. That little boy
cannot sit next to the window,
Wordsworth.

Honey, stop sending all those postcards
from Africa with lions and tigers
on them! You always send the same
cards on every trip and now
the children hardly notice anymore.
Where is Thumbkin Where is
Thumbkin? The elephant and
the African baby with no pants
on surrounded by giant bananas
gct only a passing glancc.
Here I am! Here I am! the children
and I are beautiful and my
disposition may improve. Did you
hear me? I said that if I
went to Morocco again I would
not be afraid of those mad drivers
and would not insult them. Have those
labor leaders ever stopped
talking about how awful I was compared
to you? When they handed me those bits
of lamb with their fingers in that giant
tent where the dagger dancers danced
I ate those bits and didn't ask for more.

Three or four hours later
I am sitting in Washington Square Park
and that neon light is bearing down.
All right I've made a terrible mistake
that course is terrible!
the professor doesn't teach
he just compares editions!
O Professor X!
and your "avert your eyes
while I get up on the radiator
to pull down the shade" — —
that was the most interesting thing
you said from four to six!

Take the Seventh Avenue subway
up to Columbia to hear Mark talk
on King Lear and his Comforters.
Mark is against the position
of the Christian moralists
who see in Lear a king's redemption
and the Existentialists who put him in
a garbage pail. Art cold, Fool?
I don't know why I love that line so much.
You read Lear or see it
and the reaction can be educated
but still spontaneous.

After Mark's talk I take a taxi to
the 125th street station and wait
for the 10:35 among some drunks and
a sober priest reading *The Post*
(at least I don't think it's *The
Daily News*) I put my hand in my
pocket which is full of small smooth
beige acorns which John gave me
yesterday to keep forever.

THE FLYING GLOVE

for Larry Fagin

The next time
I go to a reception
and see a lonely
person deserted in the
midst of an orange
sentence I'll say
to the socially smooth
deserter, "Hey, you, Monsieur,
you would never leave a
plane in mid-flight,
you coward. And flying
is good conversation."
Instead of being
received at receptions
we are rejected in mid-
sentence and we are
all sentenced to
endlessness, which like being
ejected from a plane
in mid-flight, is a
lonely feeling. As it is,
we who are not successes are
small bright punctured
parachutes or shrivelled
lettuce leaves. Recently
at a reception I told
the Ambassador from Gowumbi
to the U.N. that my friend
had gone to Tanzania to help
the women develop
their role. "Help, help— —
you Americans always think

you're helping somebody!"
He stormed becoming terrifying
like a tribal chief with an
Oxford accent which he is
and I became a lettuce leaf
so he abandoned me to his
mistress, a nice but stupid
girl from Brooklyn, who asked
about the children, which raw
vegetables rarely have
so I had little to say.

I think I'll empty
all the unfilled promises
I am. In my dreams a flying
glove calls to an unopened
parchute falling through
air. Have you tried
poetry? the glove calls.
Yes, I have, cries the desperate
parachute, but the poetry
editor at "The Commonweal"
rejected my eternal poem
about spring. But he is a
kind, religious man, calls back
the glove. That's true.
He did say, Try again.
Well, you must! Do you think I
have time? The parachute still
unopened still falling, the ground
growing larger and more receptive
all the time. The parachute
suddenly inspired, puts on the
glove and shouts, I'll write one
this minute and drop
it plop
on the head
of the Ambassador from Gowumbi

at a reception
and he can give it to
his mistress
for Christmas!

And so with my
Merry Christmas poem
my parachute opens
and I am a success at this
reception with no real
persons present only
facades to be
defeated by whole
sentences and my poems
become the periods at
the end of their sentences.
I boldly sing caviar and
champagne poems
revealing my ignorance
of Africa, my sloppy
French and my terrible
philosophy with its absolute
period for a Final End
to their false starts.
I have made one concession
to my closest friend and
adviser, the glove.
I hide my short unpolished
finger nails. Now I
always wear gloves
to receptions. This is
a good general rule to
follow: always wear gloves.
But the gloves must be
puffy white silk
parachutes that will land
you lightly on top of a
clump of half-declarative

half-exclamatory bushes.
It's a good idea too to
always wear a puffy white
parachute smile
and if you say nothing
all the facades will think
you're stuck in mid-flight with
them in polished French
finger nailed mid-sentence
all subject, no object
above your invisible lonely
plain pink hands.

Stop screaming
for snowpants that do not exist.
The yard is white with snow
and absolutely still.
Mary Anne, the snowpants
that you desire
are not here
not here in the reality of the living room
nor out there
in the wild white hair
of the lilac tree. Perhaps I'm blind.

Carmen Elgazu was a compendium
of all the virtues. But
she said to the seminarian, Kiss me hard
very hard.
Is virtue love of the other
and vice an egotist?
Existence might have been. . .
I hope the rose.
Will my frozen refractory daughter
desire among desires Emmanuel
and will I envy her?

CHRISTMAS

i

It's not easy
to be sincere with you.
I keep avoiding
who you are. There were no kings
or star. It irritates me to admit
these things. I've been looking
for Isaiah in department stores and

ii

wondering what
I've lost. My conversation
sticks
like a star
in my throat. Emotions,
please sit down over there
in that brown, firm chair. If only existence
were becoming

iii

what you are! The moon
is full, an oratorio
that I'll not be, not
in this world. But I hear
there is another. I hear
the Christmas Oratorio being played. The chorale,

iv

the end, is glorious, Noël.

THE RISTORANTE SAN MARCO

We are sitting here at a corner table at the
        Ristorante San Marco on 55th street.
I haven't been in a restaurant like this in quite a while.
After ordering lasagna, I look around and see that there are
        a great many elderly people here
all happy, wealthy and well-dressed.
They are all French or English or distinguished
        in some way.
The man who is sitting at the next table
        will die soon;
he is quite old
        but still he is happy
only smoothing out his jacket when he stands up to go.

These old people must have lived through sad experiences:
        death of parents, for instance,
        and the disappointment of children;
although they are rich, they may not be as eminent
        or as rich
        as they once hoped
and still they have borne it well —
        they are all laughing!

A glamorous blonde woman over there is posing.
She has slippery eyes like paramecia
        but she is not aware of it.
If only she were aware of it!
I don't think I am jealous but when she holds up
        a lorgnette in order to read her menu
I am glad.

There is a big woman on the other side of the room
        with a big black dress on.
Her husband is quite a bit smaller
        but they also are laughing.

The laughter rumbles in the small cheerful restaurant.
A painting of the Piazza San Marco in Venice is on
        the opposite wall.
The piazza does not appear flooded which is
        the way I remember it.
It looks flat and shiny like an ice skating rink
        above which Venetian clouds are accumulating
        in a false blue sky.

I can't sketch because
        I didn't bring a sketchbook.
Writing down a few observations seems like a
        sensible thing to do
although no one else in the restaurant is doing this.
We might be talking if you weren't almost sleeping.

A lot of little bottles are lined up behind me.
Brolio Bianco, little white soldiers to the left of me.
Vinrosa Birtolli, little red soldiers to the right.
You said, "March ahead and discover his theories"
        and "Success is a problem."

I have eaten all the meat in the lasagna
        and have left the pasta.
        I am not hungry.
        It looks like the Piazza di Spagna.

GARE DU NORD

for Barbara Hatch

to keep on running away or toward as if I am
standing in the gray excitement of
the Gare du Nord waiting for the train to
Denmark and the possibility of Russia now moving
toward the east and strangeness slowly and the
excitement of being stuck in close connection with
the persons in this compartment the world
exploded yesterday and we are running
a race of promises we are and I am
the south and old New Orleans moving north and bringing
you, New York, the spring my spring the color of
bananas and the soft taste of sugar cane from Napoleon
Avenue to Fifth Avenue in February having
no further concern beyond bringing the warmth of my
birth to your northern mind nothing beyond being
a wheel of tenderness wrapped in May yellow and
green crepe paper moving down Fifth Avenue bringing
love and almost everything but promises I promise
nothing but spring trees moving north and east in the
train of my thought full of cherry blossoms for
you and all of you the home of my August birth in
New Orleans is gone but that one time I was
hiding behind the hedge my grandfather
threw out Aunt Virginia's handsome black sheep
baritone Irish Philadelphia husband
Bob threw him out of the house for the last
time artistic Virginia lacked practicality I was
just like her everyone said and now I have arrived here
where all the brown sticks of winter are
shining a southern wheel moving in the north of
my experience giving you everything but
my recipe for poulet au gratin which I have

lost and may have lost much else besides may have
little left to give and I am running
away or toward or both it's Lent which means
a race Saint Paul implied being an athlete few very few
will win in doubt in turning I return to
summer and dark ages by the sea of mutual memory we are
who were two children standing by the wild
Atlantic in striped beach capes we imagined ourselves
queens how they flew at four o'clock

JULY AT DAWN

for Nancy Carolan, Catherine Cleary,
Claire Kennedy, Margaret Snyder

1

Last night in this unusual room
the stars flickered and
went out with the moon
with finality I pulled down
the shade lay down
on the hot black coals
of the night and dreamed
of pyramids

2

I understand the Twiga
Hotel and that you will be
there with them
in Dar Es Salaam
and my jealousy my brief
longings will be here with these children
these creations of

3

weekends after Africa!
Fourth of July weekend
Labor Day weekend
and two others I forget

4

White with rage the sun
composes noon after noon

31

after noon with no
periods

5

Lean out the warm window: dawn
leaning on green
leaves green apples
green Pentacost chasubles
the intellectual immature priest
and the July dawn sky
like the skin of a peach

6

and fall back
"there was ten things under the bed
and I did those ten things and
there was ten things not
under the bed and I
did those ten
things" he said

7

above the beach
the pale yellow sky
is an illuminated map
on which navy blue clouds
are continents outlined
by lightning

8

on a Boston beach
three girls were sitting all night

waiting for the sun
after sophomore year
to roll triumphant over
the sea just like their philosophy

look
here it comes
I cried

9

oh dawn
of brides and old alleluias!

AFTER BREAKFAST ON AUGUST 21ST

for Anne Waldman

yet one cannot accept that after all
we did for Banda summoning him from the
wilds and making him our leader could he
hope to run that country alone not being
a Red but like Horowitz a Catholic of the
most undogmatic irresistable kind some-
thing like an Arabian American if that
conjures up empty restaurants on vacancies
for the summer when Corning dies only to
rise again the new New York and the old
African lying there in the trunk of the
elephant's shade forever nouveau forever
a nephew to a multimillionaire is a clear-
cut New Yorker where my poems have
only an abstract innocence careening
wildly lookout she's coming!
and will eternally remain like the smell of
a Parisian skunk under the cabin on the
river Schroon where adolescence is always
the perfect vision of a tanned lagoon

of a feminine dressing table born of
an orange crate covered with chintz and
now one must finally admit the depressive
demon that has haunted Mipembere through-
out California for the attention of Mrs.
Grace Pokani the first Wassaland girl every to
pass needlework and other developing
countries the train goes so slow and
sometimes so fast like life like
Willie like an imprisoned will power

like a kitchen in which all of life
goes down and comes up the drain
like a lizard oh I have accidentally
caught the most purposeful truth
in the story of a lizard on
a Moyen Atlas mountain a Benedictine
lizard falling out of the faucet and
rising toward the window of Holy Saturday so
cold so impregnable so totally like
relative war that we are all committed to
confessing that our favorite saint is an
astronaut and his favorite the most
developed girl from an old nation

so no one is ever free is ever
able to believe that getting into
orbit is not quite as critical as the
broken television aerial lost in
flight in the parental fight for the
heroic child the harrowing dream of the
launch phase above the earth where
all of their children are giving themselves
the extra little push that is no longer
necesary because they are in that ring
of light the beautiful recovery area above
Bermuda and past efforts to be admitted to
the Merrill Palmer School in Detroit but
now I am engaged in the struggle of that humble
but great man so I have to hurry because there are
no scholarships left for the tea party
I have fallen asleep again and
it's only after breakfast after ten
after the second Saturday after
my thirty-seventh birthday on earth and I
am prepared to play that tape for you
now: Mrs. Smith cannot have any
more children because her father died

the child said and knew that the cellar
door is locked and wait awhile for Père Feret
who has been accompanying Abraham on his
trip to the ark with David
Jordan a specialist in the familiarity
of which we are all jealous

Gregory of Nyssa says and I believe him
because I feel that I cannot go on like this
leaning on my elbows forever not
actually sick but unable to stand
up remembering with this most bruised
memory how Heliodorus was scourged
by the angels and why is it that
I of all persons living and dead
am not afraid anymore I can't
show this to anyone because the whole
Mipembere thing is very sensitive
and has a relation to unreality so
the directions are to walk straight
ahead and continue not to care about
the Malawi problem then you are not
ideological and will eventually win
the key to the cellar full of ideas
and temporary jobs for those who are
buoyed up by the completion of
breakfast under a burnt ceiling caused
by a peach who would not limit her
activity to temporal matters

what is true of each one of us
is also true of Jimmy who
remains very subjective lost in the
intricacies of his inception
the jack-knife bridge opening
the ore boats the wheat barges passing
through et erat mater laughing!

desolate and lone and smoking cheroots
with Pancho Villa and wrote letters
to O'Hare who suddenly left with another
woman on Saturday night just when we were
going to play bridge and he alone lacked
diapers and other covering but still
maintaining a protective radiance
that lasted throughout the day and on into
Sunday when suddenly we were all terrible
and old and summer ran cold and what are we going
to do now after eleven o'clock if you think
you are writing a poem in order to escape
from your chores you had better face the
tragedy of being a forerunner and misunderstood

you ha!
since you came back from your trip
yesterday I feel totally irresponsible
please understand the summer is almost
over and nothing has been fun not folk
dancing in the parking lot not McDonaldburgers
at the beach not cigarettes lighting the
old dreams of campfires where the
most beautiful poems I ever wrote when
I was ten were read aloud
and loved as the new topping on the sundae
street is encouraged to be confident and
brave the threats of constant study and the loss
of safety pins so I can go on imitating
a poem I couldn't understand as if every
unseen word must be typed in order to be
forgiven nothing was fun not those
Saturday afternoons at the beach among
the breasts and hips that roll in waves
or the sea straight as the back
of a boy or the imitation of my face
in round white paper plates

and nothing can be helped
not finding a dress on sale buying it although
too big and not becoming still it was new I
thought and still think newness and
the desire for it can make one mad
enough to spend one's life searching
as some spend it looking for fog
and little psalms to carry them away
to the tent of an indian named sunrise
and the great god of thumbs

the trouble with me is that I can't
understand whether I am the lamplight
or one of the two people underneath it
not that I have any choice
in the core of an apple is a plum Adam
thought or said he thought it's summer
and warm and there'd be no harm the little
crayfish in the red paper cup in the kitchen
is dead and I dread the dispersal of my
hopes all twelve of them the grocer
delivered because of my twelve lunch guests
a white cat slips over the porch when I
ring the brass bell all of the children
come with more crayfish in paper cups when
the guests are due with no underwear or
sneakers on things seem to be getting worse
but who cares what I believe a rat will go on
pilgrimage and the frog stands still
an example of action versus
contemplation which is better ah my dear
friend says the country mouse and that is my
answer friendship is best and the worst sinner
is the bat who does not throw in his lot
with either party preferring to sit on
the beach alone drinking coke and imagining
that he is an illustration for the Inferno

slow and steady wins the race
O'Hare! and Hatch is an action name and
Bloom is a foreign garden memorable although
unvisited perhaps and Ferrari is sleek speed
which I do not own and cannot become
in this woodcut I am a part of by
Antonio Frasconi the twelve-toed jay part
stunned and wobbly in a balanced mood
under my burning coat

WAITING

for Annette Hayn

waiting
the winter   of distances   comes
                  like little onions   somewhat greyish
                  pink, with vague vertical stripes
                  expanding at the horizon, yet motionless
perhaps I've done something wrong
                  should have telephoned someone
I see faces   old school, new school
I hear   a flock of small   rains
I hear   nothing, the tick of it
                  has come into my room
unchanged
I'll wait again   tomorrow

BRIDGE

for my sister

where are you going
nowhere   same as you

a beautiful hard journey
eight steps down
and ten across. . .

bring all the provisions
for the river is intricate
and the bridge moves slowly

a shiny red car
on the other side
is going the other way

it's as I remembered
the dream
I keep on

my sweater my coat my gloves
to protect my rough memory
from the ferry   the sightseers
the white foam story

along my way
I sat down and died
beside a bright canal

ZENIZENABO

What is it that anyone is
since the first grade or earlier?
Or in a Swiss village several generations ago?
Or in the Italian Alps in the fourth century?
I wonder at what stage of the world I grew into
this word.

I wonder in a mystical way, perhaps,
if we are seen in different mirrors by different persons.
The way I see you, for instance, has nothing to do with spring.
It has been raining for a long time, in the secret cemetery,
before I was awake, before the formation of the stars
and of thinking.

I know what you are thinking:
that I am drinking a magic potion.
Yet someone sees me as a hooded revolutionary
and someone else, as a specialized bohemian,
coming out of the woods on Sunday, in late afternoon,
with a collection.

I know what you are thinking:
that I am drinking a magic potion.
Yet someone sees me as a hooded revolutionary
and someone else, as a specialized bohemian,
coming out of the woods on Sunday, in late afternoon,
with a collection.
And at another time, in a sailor dress,
the conscience of all Kensington.

When I look up from my typewriter for just a minute,
I see fir trees that belong to me.
And the lining of a jacket on the floor becomes
legendary under the sun's red flannel feet.

The phone has rung three times this morning.
The first was a child, the second a friend,
and the third was the voice of my father.

Are drums beating the horizon?

Eventually, too soon, the leaves and the indians will go away.
Then the horizon will go and you, too.
Anyway, there's someone I have to telephone right now, so goodbye!
I like rusty chrysanthemums, tambourines flung heavenward,
and stony walls. Yet we are born to be free.
So, it is possible to hate all of these things
and to want others.

At this point in the meditation, the stereo begins to play
Zenizenabo, a courage song for warriors.

POSTCARD

to Catherine Murray

I'm having a good time
at this monastery!

I brought along James Joyce
and Virginia Woolf.
But I'm at home here anyway.
Oh, Regina Laudis, queen of praise,
mother! You don't know this green

hill. There's pain
in the cloister. But I'm not there yet,
I don't leave until Friday.
Right now, he is laid out upstairs
in a twisted sheet, a murderous
mummy. I am circling the kitchen. And the children
have gone to a carnival.

ST. STEVEN'S DAY. DAWN

They are throwing stones
at St. Steven and I'm going to die!

From my silver car
I see broken branches

and renewed blackbirds
praying over poinsettias of saints.

Above the street
he hugs his lighted martyrdom.

I hear the chained bridegroom
clapping the waking wheels of his snow bride.

the
city
of
God
and
the
city
of
man
are
the
same
city
more
gay
more
miserable
the
skyline
is
falling
I
go
home
alone
I
go
home
with
Apollinaire
rain
is
falling
on
my
four
silver
bracelets
how
strange
life
is
nothing
we
can
touch

KISUMU: A DREAM

Do you remember Kisumu
        where we were like lamplight together?
Black Herons   Purple Herons   Night Herons
        I will never forget those nights!

Remember the lavender leopards
        and the gold goats straying into
the wild twilight sky of Kisumu
        just before we went on?

The luminous past is dim now
        soon Fish Eagles will be flicking our bones.
Oh, Kisumu! My dream of light, only light!
        And you: you were a Great White Heron.

ODE TO NEW YORK

1

When I pass you at night
your shade is down
when I pass you in the morning
your shade is up
curtains flying like wings

2

The subway screams
and staggers
my fears have fallen or jumped
I lean against
the orange railing of the subway stairs
the first noon of February
suddenly opens up
and becomes a day of oranges

3

Two thin young men
are leaning toward each other in a sooty doorway
one is trying to get something
out of the eye of the other
with a white handkerchief and great delicacy

4

At sunset your sky's a stone altar
of sacrifice
blood is spilling

through the grilled arms
of Central Park

5

You are a pregnant woman
you carry me upside down

6

I wait for a bus
a drunk pushes his elbow
into my chest

the bus drums loudly
my silence reaches a new pitch

reality is trash!

7

I look out of
a high window of ambition
I'm a lighted prisoner
dancing in your orchard
of tall lemon trees

8

On a circular stage
the wild girl
born in a ditch
is raped by the prisoners
and then made modest
by the quest. . .
Poets and madmen!
I rush to the stage

49

9

New York, my winter stars
fall onto your jagged shoulders
and into your pockets
they are my poems
keep them! keep them!

SATURDAY LIST

1. Jim to Tommy G.'s birthday party at three
2. Buy Loony Links
3. Death in a dark shop
4. These pickles are delicious and not sour as she said
5. Find someone to murder me
6. Finally, the chest of the doomed soldier began to heave
    with a strange motion. It increased in violence until
    it was—

    Larry, are you there?

    as if an animal were within
    kicking and tumbling furiously—

    Larry!

    to be free

7. Haircut at five
8. Takc shower now
9. The snow circles the horizon and cannot land
10. Astro will come and save us
11. Take off your bathrobe, nightgown and sneakers
12. Toby called the Africans. "This is it."
13. The snow is kicking and tumbling furiously
14. Go to the A & P
15. The Jubilation
    by John the Evangelist

    I said, John, I remember
    your birth

    John, I said, don't leave me

(The Evangelist
as a boy of six)

16. I am the
    poet of
    morality
    and immorality
    all heroes
    of the imagination
    come
    to
    me

17. The Evangelist said,
    Huckleberry, are you somewhere in the kitchen?
    Come out, Huckleberry

18. I have no hope
    all the room long
    I have searched the afternoon
    the dark wife
    the butcher shop

19. Before you die
    send loving letters
    to your friends

20. Also violent ones

21. I have already spoken. . .I have
    a statement. . .and he in his flowery
    voice said no

22. Send the perfect dream
    that I wait for in flowers

23. you
    know
    not

how
wretched
your daughter
is
Lysistrata
said
(and sinks down exhausted)

24. and yet
the world
is worthy
of the gods

the snow
invents them

25. 839-6083
Larry, are you there?

26. This is the end

27. The water
is beating
on my head

28. What can I say?

29. We were together in Berlin

30. The snow
is floating
upward
like a
tree

FIREWORKS

1. Make enough salad dressing this time.
   It's beautiful outside.
   Why don't you come out?

   I can't get used to it.
   I can't get used to life.

   He said, We must move with the times.
   These were his last human words.

2. Come on outside. It's lovely.
           as the monsoon weather lifted slightly
   fly strikes close to the base perimeter
   Red River docks   Red River
           as the monsoon weather
   checked by what they had witnessed
           lifted slightly
   has not stopped the flow of men
              into the Red River   the Red River

3. Many of the young people in our community
   do not have a real understanding of business.
   You can encourage them by . . .

   I'm going to kill your son!

   Oh, yeah!

4. Yellow rays stretch down through enormous gentle clouds
   over the endless parking lot.

   No, you can't have a balloon!

I want to say yes
stretch out along my littered shore. . .

5. You know, he's got himself trained so that he can
do anything in less than a minute.

6. The doorbell rings at 4 a.m.

Rickie will find out that I am gone.
Georgie will find out that you are gone.
Then they'll really start to worry about us!

7. If Humphrey is as good for Daley
as Daley is for Humphrey,
it will be a great day for Chicago!

8. They say I look twenty-five?
Do you want me to make that dessert again?
You are writing that damn poem.
Daddy is forty.
Not how old I am but how old I look.
Daddy looks in the high twenties or low thirties.
I am not forty!
God is colorless.

9. On the beach
we ate small cool hamburgers and drank watery root beer.
No one could write a poem there.
The beating of the drums, the beat, beat, beat!
The crowd loved it.

10. Beyond Nietzsche, Feuerbach and Heidegger
beyond the romantic poets Richter and de Nerval
the theme of the death of God is almost two centuries old.
The recurrent image is that the sun has disappeared.

11. We have to be uprooted from everything.
I rebel!

Ethel Kennedy looks blankly down
at her husband's coffin.
The beach will open officially tomorrow.
Sailboats move softly out to sea.
Family life is a terrible thing—
          only after Mau Mau did Kenya achieve—
Sails are white vestments of
priests on some strange new
pathway to
the dead.

12. I can't figure out who is responsible
for this fight that everyone is in
in the living room.
This sense of being blocked.

I have an idea.
You go over and see Mike and Dot.
We'll eat dinner.
Otherwise, it will get too late
and the children will miss the fireworks.

I am wondering if there is something
else I might do, might run as excited poet
for president, might climb a rather low
mountain and swing gently from a willow
over the cliffs—

My Boy Scout camp list
is not your top drawer.

. . .might take a train to California and be
alone except for the passengers
I meet who will along with the scenery
I have never seen inspire the best
poems of the age which I will write—

Come on! When are we going to go?

. . .might be a dancer. I who am afraid to dance
but am at heart a great dancer.

13. Dad said for you to go and see the Colemans
    and bring them here.
    The fireworks will begin at nine o'clock.

    Do you know what the Fourth of July means?
    Who was fighting whom?
    I knew something about my country when I was your age.

    When Martin Luther King was killed—
    I drank sweet vermouth
    and smoked until my mouth burned.

14. The fireworks will begin soon!

    It's lightning that's bright in Ghelderode.

    But when are we going to eat?
    Dad's mad.
    You have to go to the Carrs right now!

    Barabbas says: Now is the hour of the oppressed.
    The clown kills Barabbas with a tiny knife.

15. Forty years old, I tell you.
    A sad day, eh?

    The fireworks will begin in fifteen minutes!

    I always believed
    I would have a destiny
    a wonderful destiny
    and in this childish belief
    I was just like you.

    Dad wants to know why
    you didn't serve the salad.

But that's not the question now.
We must move with the times.

(Rhinoceros heads fill the upstage wall.
From left to right in the house, the noise
of running feet and the panting breath of the
animals.)

We have to go! We're leaving now!

The Gallaghers left. The Dunns left.
The Colemans left. The Carrs left. The Csenges left.
The Barberos left. The Larsens left.
The Fullers left. The Cohens left.
Monsignor Delaney left. Father Raich left.
The Hatches left. The Selbys left. The Von Oehsens left.
Rabbi Kertzer left. The Rosenbergs left.

We missed the fireworks last year!

(A noise of stamping. Plaster falls from the ceiling.
The house shakes violently.)

You're done! Your poem is done! Come on.

July 4, 1968

THE BLUE AND YELLOW
for Charles North

I'm in a blue and yellow
mood. Blue as the dead
sea and yellow as a falling star.
There is no one to collect my
garbage, the refuse of a too active
imagination remains stinking in my mind.

I've tried everything, including
gin and tonic but still I hate
everyone and will do nothing kind
or sincere.

I'm a summer rose turned black,
the creepy ears of a rhododendrun.
I should love poets, but even they
have become surplus goods, something
I have in my attic. What to do with
all this junk? It takes more energy
than I have, I tell you.

Ezra says, Prepare to go on a journey.
What advice from a great soothsayer!
I know I have to drive to the eternal
log cabin in Vermont. I know
I have to wait for a whole woods of wolves
in my nights. To eat me up? I'd rather
live, a leftover salad, than be dead.
Every summer I think: this is the end.
Someone has just said: stupid idiot.

Should I punish him? Should I care? Certainly
not. I agree with him. He is absolutely
right, as Boy Scouts have some dirty aspect
of truth, the truth of sneakers, sleeping
bags and badges. This is life.

How I hate life! But I refuse to die!

I have been embroiled in wars
long enough. It's not enough to hate
one's friends. It is not enough to
wish they would all be dethroned from
their dreams. Sure, I wanted
to be queen, a beautiful queen, revered
by the populace. I would like to bring
justice to all, not love. After all,
I have passed through the valley
of Westchester and swam the Shelldrake
alone. Charon didn't guide me. No one
guided me. I simply whispered to the
water that I was there and it moved. So
perhaps I am really a goddess, whose speech
is a rainbow uniting all the wicker chairs
of the world.

I am a student of the times
willing to write anything as long as
it is confusing and not what anyone
needs. I condemn you to drink the milk
of a camel. Drink it!
It's bad for you, as I will be too.
I am tired of being sophisticated.
It was just a pose. A scared rabbit's
imitation of Superman. We will not speak of
religion and the diseased ideas of

nuns, who are condemned to be good women,
too good. What is wrong with a good woman?
She doesn't go far enough. She shrinks.
She tightens.

Well, what am I? The mother of the next
generation? The wind between the mountains,
the bell of a train on a night curve?
What am I, then, sister to tigers
and avalanches? What do I want to destroy?
Shall I never dance on the surf of
a party, free as the ocean in the arms
of a spray, rising upward and forward with
a great roar? I might frighten somebody
timid. I'm not a lake in Vermont where
I am fated to go, where the water is flat,
an icy responsibility.

What must I do, Father? Leave him
out of it! Yes, I do wish to go abroad
on a ship. I wish to meet with all of
the cannibals of Europe, what wild beasts
I may talk with at the Louvre, or just
outside it at a café. No one can imagine
having a gentle man for president. Where
are our masks? But it doesn't matter because
Nigeria is being born again in the bowels of
New York, and you are a midwife, ever
zealous and patient. All that is here
are demons who intend to celebrate the
end of my life and yet there is someone
who gives me an offering of life
contained in a box made of ice
cream sticks pasted over with blue feathers.
From the wreckage of dolls, I bring
this moonstone away. I am the last survivor

and I want to speak in the name of
joy, the joy lost somewhere along
the river to be found among
the blue and yellow of it all.

from *VACATION IN VERMONT*

Sixth Day (August 21, 1968)

We drive up a high hill
and look at four mountains.
The longer we look
the more peaceful we are
until the boys knock over
the haystacks.
Then I shout at them
and you walk angrily down
the hill and red tracer bullets
soar over Hradcany Castle
overlooking Prague
and heavy small arms fire
—the laughter of children
among the haystacks—
pick them up!—
is heard on the bank
of the Vltava River.
A white artillery flare
rose over the castle.
We have come so far
on this road safely
and the peace is broken
by anger—and I wonder why
you left me alone
waiting for the boys
whose shouts echo on the hilltop
and one comes crying
from the haystacks
with a bloody lip.
And in the tread
of one of the tanks
is embedded
a pink shoe.

VUETBAN

> that's a typographical error
> this poem is a mistake

Here is a poem that has a lot to offer
because it is endless
and, in order to achieve its object,
must fail artistically, otherwise,
it will not be of use.
If it does not seem to be
about Vuetban at times
it is still there
terrible and endless
being written late at night. . .
Here we are . . .

> in Vuetban
> another error, this calculated, in order
> to lose more lines.

Three sons already dead in Vuetban
Aged 12, 9 and 5 —
I can't allow this
to happen!
Madam, will you please
leave? You are causing
a disturbance.
Come on, boys, I said, lets
get out of here.

A young priest comes in
and blesses the house

and before you know it
something terrible happens
and then something more terrible.

An old woman in many layers of gold clothing
waddles down Fifth Avenue muttering
Impeach Rockefeller!
Everyone gives her a strange look
and finally we are all strange
and she is our leader. . . . .

ii.

A canoe came.
          I was an Indian.
I got in
          and paddled all the way to

                    Vuetban

Nobody knew I was coming.
The old gang from college was there — not too happy
          to see me
and no one seemed happy to see me.

Anyone that preoccupied with herself
cannot do justice to Vuetban!

Vuetban may not exist
because I am going
on vacation
to an island
in the ocean. . .

I am beginning to doubt
that I can write this poem forever.

I come from a long line of philosophers
trained in the Judeo-Christian ethic
which is, that you must help people
to extinguish themselves
and that is just what I've done!

I am a success!
Vuetban does not exist!
Goodnight!

1970–1980

MODERN TIMES

Time is falling through me
so fast I can't catch it.
All night the foghorn blows
the minutes into my ear.
Time dives into the waves
and catches me by the legs.
Time is behind the black rock.
Find him! Find him!
Look, I know what you're after —
but you can't have it!
Take my blue ring, my green beads —
take these raisins and nuts
from a pretty girl!
Here's the bluefish of midnight
for the worst journeys!
the living crab, the Christ
hidden in a boat! Time
bites my arm. The light in
the lighthouse is out. The sandpiper
ran away. I'd like to
ride over Time on a bike
and twist his neck in a flag.
But what good would that do?
I've missed the great breakers.
And these babies died too soon.
Time didn't notice them but
the orange sky above the
historic cemetery is beautiful
and newly born
and the spinster whose brother just died
is laughing, the feverish little boy
is laughing and imitating Chaplin,

the poet whose father left home when
he was five is laughing, the drunk
who is asleep is laughing, the blue
bathing suit is laughing, the plane
crash dream is laughing, the vacation
that is over for good is laughing
the smashed clock whose hour hand
is limp but the minute hand goes on
ticking the future is laughing

GHOSTS

Here is the ghost of the unknown wife
happy as the statue of liberty
Here is the ghost of parents
driving south for good
to a colorful foreign country
that is a ghost in the memory
of a child who will always be a ghost child

Here is the ghost of love
dark and drooping lips of deep rooted rhododendrons
Here is the ghost of peace reduced to a pink and gold banner
Here is the ghost of all sweaters
yellow blue and green sweaters sweaters of the earth
moonlit sweaters of young daughters

Here is the ghost of the smile of the red leaf shadow of change
the ghost of a bomb as it falls and spreads a starfish
on the beach of the world
the ghost of two orange candles eating themselves up
the ghost of september september the beat of the wicked child's drum
beating the time of tears of ghosts of soldiers who look and wait

Here is the ghost of the beautiful fish of Christ
never caught
the ghost of the moon in the white football helmet tossed in the air
the ghost of the future as a child scribbles his identity
the ghost of life in the playhouse
where broken-down things are the ghosts of perfection
the ghost of a husband
in the purple air
the ghost of all conversation
in the dialogue of Chekhov

where card playing becomes the escape
from the flea-ridden orange cat
the ghost of the dentist's exciting dream
of being everywhere in the world at once
the ghost of possibility in the little red wooden car
that waits at my door
the ghost of eternity of travel of dressing of brushing your teeth
the ghost of the smallest possession a silver ring
the last one left the one that you remember in the grave
where you become the ghost of man
ghost of my ghost

THE ISLE OF THE LITTLE GOD

in memory of my father

        My first wish
is to be alone but
not lonely, to go beyond
the solemn high
        mass of the
breakers to something simple
not frightening.
Outside our cottage
an old father sings
a mournful tune to
his baby and a yellow
kite vanishes.
        No escaping
the card tricks, the King of
Hearts. Do you know the secret?
Your man is trapped.
Only one move
will save him.
        This island wind
is uncovering. Jim blows
an eternal whistle. We take
it away. Then he whistles
through his teeth.
        Let's leave out
some of the words. Tell me
the lie you were going
to tell me.
        Listen, I am
brushing my teeth.
Jane's blackberry pie
is in the oven. I dream
I am a big woman

trying to squeeze into
a small coffin.
The pie crust doesn't look
done. The sea commits me
to absolutely nothing.
It is too gracious
to make demands.
Shipwrecked sailors held on
and on.
      Children run in
from the blackberry patch
full of irreligious innocent
stains. We rode through
a cloud, told ghost stories and
saw a lot of bats. Did
you see the tombstones shining
after the gale? an old man
cried to me.
      Paul says, "I'm an adult
going into ninth grade.
I'm not a sex maniac anymore."
Across the fields a horse
runs wild.
      I look for
high trees of protection
on this island but I can't
find any. Ambushed indians
jumped off the bluffs
into the arms of
the little god. When
people die, I don't know
what to say to them.
The green light of my eyes
of the lighthouse is twirling.
The green whistle, the green
kite, the green cottage
the green life
is changing color

THE LAMP

The gray smoke of lamps, keys, pennies, of lightning. . .
The dull stars no one notices anymore
Red leaves in old age, most beautiful right before death
Two clocks   two alarms   two hesitations   true or false
On the school wall sits my son
        the prisoner whose rays are being extinguished
I know   I know
My shoes are a disappointment to me too

You can't pull an image too close
It might hurt
You might have to call an ambulance
It is silent now
Tonight in my blue lampshade
I am sort of an old bride
The bride of London, Copenhagen and Berlin
I have married the best masculine cities
So I am not alone with a smashed lamp
to whom I was the shade and sun

5 A.M.

It is 5 a.m. Sunday November 14th and all the streets
        have tied up their hair in small knots
Paul is not in his bed
At this very moment Apollinaire is making inquiries for me at the
        all-night doughnut shop
I am in the costume of an ancient choir boy
I hear a car coming or is it a bird
Mary Anne is lying here breathing
The ceiling is shedding real tears
At the moment of death you recover your sanity
You begin to talk for the first time the world listens
A police car is stopping a policeman is talking
I'd better put a bathrobe on
Perhaps in my dream the moon has been delivered
the groceries include a star
I'll look in the mirror one more time
As one generation is sacrificed
the next builds an altar
and the next covers it with carnations
Now three generations are knocking at the door at once
There's a hurricane outside the water is rising
The clown answers
        and comforts each with a laugh

1. Those who are closest to me
   are an orange light a warning
   that the circus of Christmas
   is coming on stilts so high
   I can't see it
   but the white-washed face
   of a clown speaks as
   the blonde maiden
   on a donkey is dragged
   with a balloon in her belly
   slowly through the sawdust
   and the black ballet dancer
   stretches upward grotesquely
   his hands made by hand
   by his cruel older sister
   poor pip poor anne
   and card tricks dance
   with faces upside down
   the ringmaster calls out
   that Christ is born
   and we know that this is
   our ambition to create
   a dream bible of the imagination
   some quasi-religious thing
   a parade beginning with
   a gigantic skeleton
   of the first man
   the serpent will probably be
   very helpful in this

2. Shem's wife jumped through
        a green hoop

              and was gone
Ham's wife somersaulted
              through a pink hoop
              and was gone
Japeth's wife somersaulted
              through a yellow hoop
              and was gone
the Ringmaster is attentive
              and honestly doesn't know
the Offertory Dance
              will begin at once
although the acrobat is now detached
the one I did understand
              was Noah's wife
she wanted to stick around
she wouldn't get into the Ark

3. Now the new poets are too young
    and the middle-aged poets too famous
    my poem couldn't move
              for a couple of days
    because my bones were dry
    I was mainly interested
              in the Creation
    got carried away
              by an angel
    who told me ambition
    was not nice in a woman
    if I'm forced to leave
              the train
              due to a catastrophe
    I can pick up a son
              outside a phone booth
              outside the police station
    I can examine the curved gilt pipe
    I can remember
              how it was to be Mary
              having her first son

I was a fluorescent flower
now I don't know my role
don't know my son
lost somewhere on the road
from Bethelehem to hell
it seems like the history of Herod
"Forgive me." For what?
"I don't know."
This is the medicine
        of the Lord Jesus—
a dagger in the heart
a cross in the head
please mention my name in heaven
even my father is new there this year
I am the juggler
he didn't understand
still he loves me I guess

4. If you don't get out of this train soon
   you'll drown in the tears
           of the Serpent
   I have other plans for you
   other temptations
           of which we'll speak later
   in the meantime all those meditations
           on olive trees
           hold the truth shining silver
           interlaced with sin
   but nobody sins anymore
   sexy poems are really O.K. this Christmas
   in former times life was simple
           and more straightforward
   you were put to death
           through the Body of Christ
   you rode an elephant into the Black Sea
   I rode a camel into the Red Sea
   I am very learned
   my errors are not Christian errors

my life is ethereal
        it is an other, an otherness
        a disappearance
thus spoke Jesus
and staggered through the saw dust
Le Prince de la Paix
Venez!
because I'm alone and so is Noah

5. Rain, rain. A blonde maiden sings
   a song about rain
   If everything seems too bad
   this is the story to fall back on:
   the parade, the Final Coming
   is about to begin —
           the giant on stilts
           whose face you will never see
           who will unite the world
           the lugubrious animals
           that will make you laugh forever

   under the big top
           a band plays the ultimate gaiety
           so you'll forget that
           love alone remains
           a passionate study to be played
           on a humiliated piano
           with the left hand
           marching upward
           on the black keys
           to the earth

"The earth and all you behold although it appears without
it is within." — William Blake

THE EARTH WITHIN

I would like to speak but the river speaks through me
Let me tell you the story. . .
            No, there's thunder inside my wrist
            which makes conversation impossible

The Hudson River contains a poem of mine
that it will not give up
            Inside my brain there is a slow black dragon
            There is a woman whose whole face is a leaf

Do you remember the ointment with which Mary Magdalene. . .
The cross is woven into my green dress
I feel the cross growing

This is oblivion
the beginning
of the earth within

            as mountains are within
            you feel them move your heart
            in wider and wider circles

PSALM 90

> *for Frances Waldman*

The future will be happy although the past was sad
I see six white stallions chained to chariots
            that are going to carry away the people of the Bronx
Although it is true that everyone in the Bronx
            has grown ugly
Each citizen has put on fantastic purple robes
            and has brought his lunch with him
For the Lord is good but the trip
            may take too long
But the future is coming!

Perhaps the Lord is frustrated and angry
Maybe he was as used to wars as we are
but he grew up in a gentle home too
However, times have changed
            Mary is swearing now
            and Joseph is irrational
Well, the future will be bright, says the Lord
The sky has taken over the future
            The idea is to put the future
            on a plane and hijack it
Send the future to Cuba
            because frankly I am sick of the future already
The people of the Bronx
            are being borne slowly aloft in chariots
but they have eaten their lunches
and their purple robes aren't warm enough
so quite a few have come down with pneumonia
and the rest are starving

This has been reported to the Lord
            who is anxious to accommodate them

but negotiations are still going on
The future boils down to China or Cuba
The people of the Bronx are becoming disillusioned with the future
They are quite content with life on 200th Street
That ugly apartment house looks good to them now
Something serious is going on here
            a fight between the Lord God
            and the people of the Bronx
If it is true that the duty of every Catholic is to be a revolutionary
it is also true that the Catholics of the Bronx are not doing their duty
            in fact, they are reactionary
            many of them don't even believe in psychiatry!
Certainly the recent past has been held together
            by the psychiatrists
The Lord knows this but is helpless to do anything about it
If he tells the Catholics of the Bronx
that they are bad Catholics
he will cause an uproar and a loss of votes
And the Lord has to get reelected
So hypocrisy is the fate of the Lord

Quite a few people want to run for God
            you'd be surprised—no poets though
The trouble is the truth
The past was sad
            and the future will be sadder
and if you don't want the future
            then you don't want God
            but God loves you
            and you need love
That's logical and French
but God is not a foreigner!

I see a face that is disintegrating
If a face can disintegrate so can the creator of that face
for you can only create that which is part of yourself
and who wants the love of a disintegrating god!
I've heard that we have to have courage, we have to carry on

Bullshit, I say!
Refuse to go on!
Cancel the Resurrection and all other expectations!
Mary died alone. Lady Macbeth died alone. Cleopatra died alone.
A kiss from those lips! And then Solomon died alone.
Here is the song of Solomon:
       Venture forth from Lebanon and come to me, my bride.
       Maid of Sulam, come back, come back.
       But the maid of Sulam says goodbye
       So goodbye to the future
              goodbye, sadness
              goodbye, Bronx
              goodbye, Cuba
              goodbye, China
              goodbye, President Nixon
              goodbye, sky
              goodbye, hijackers
              goodbye, God
              goodbye, Anne, and all you people out there
              goodbye to the beautiful but ultimately false Psalm 90

1972

very softly this evening do you realize that human music always starts off softly and then the wind changes it into a dramatic confrontation the police glide in and out and Chopin continues unbaffled he ran out of the house all I saw was a tall boy in a white shirt, jeans and bare feet running beyond the bushes beyond police cars into eternity and whatever he is now doing unimaginable things and in my mind there is a crescendo of piano music for reassurance there is an order and beauty in the riddle there is a rainbow over the corner store and dipping behind the Steak N' Brew I cross the street and see a rainbow that transcends the town and the disturbing events of this evening a boy running yet it seems that he is holding up one end of the rainbow and that I am holding the other

FIERY EASTER

This is a fiery Easter!
I am the divine flame-thrower
throwing flames as far as Rome!

My flames are beds for the saints

Pope Paul leaps onto a flame
          with only a faint whine of discontent

I assure him that no priest would ever marry me

Saint Cecelia sits
          on the edge of a flame
          playing a jew's harp
          no, an Irish harp

My flames are human anger and divine beauty

Saint Paul is climbing onto a flame now
          even though I am a woman flame-thrower
          and he despises me

Santa Maria in Trastevere
          offers some excuse
          of previous plans to meditate in a private chapel
          but I assure her that Easter is fiery this year
          and that the flames can be used as prayer rugs too

I am on fire from head to foot
          burned up yet still burning
          so I belong with Abelard
          and not the saints

Yet I am not mediaevel and this is Easter morning!
    and the flames are Easter lilies
    turning into huge marigolds

St. Christopher leaps over the Tiber in one giant step
    and now rides the crest of a flame

St. Anne—I thought she must be a decrepid great-grandmother
    but here she is in a red pants suit—Hello!—
    perches sexily on the edge of a flame

Martha and Mary, the sisters,
    are fighting over the same flame

St. Joseph, in his reserved silent way, applauds the whole idea . . .

Now that I have all these saints riding on flames
Where will I take them?
There is no one I want them to meet
and I have nothing to say!

I'll send them back to their tombs
What I wanted was simply the movement of myths and realities
    and the fire
The fire of Christ
and only I who remember him
    can understand the flames

OUR TEAM

The team has broken up and fallen down. The team is a lie a sail on the horizon as the team approaches everybody picks up his towel and leaves the beach. The team is rejected! The team and the sea alone forever! Still our team will not give up the general good the general falsity will never die and the political candidate will always announce that his young wife is right here with us in the gym!

Agnostics and Communists are on our team. And our team is full of strange Christians. If only I were religious! But I am religious! Here in Heaven you have no choice. If you admit that you are an atheist, it would be suicide and our team talks about suicide but would never commit it; to be committed to death would imply a disinterest in clothes. But our team is telling me that I should be interested only in the November ideal, the Saints. The most interesting saint is St. Luke the Incorrigible, whom the school hates and the team loves. This son steals over the horizon of money and then steals over the horizon of the soul until the soul turns into lightning and the team explodes.

> St. Luke will return as the star who keeps
>   the keys to the abyss
> The ninth son will come out, brilliant, beautiful
>   and fiery red and he will be empowered to take away
>   all peace from the world
> And how are the children? asks the smiling
>   candidate as I go into the polling booth
> And I vote againsts that candidate, against that
>   smile, against that question
> Then the devil rose up out of the sea blaspheming:
>   I am the Father and the Son
> Going then in pursuit of the boy's mother
>   but she was given two wings and a red sweater

Throw out everything that says Thursday. We cannot have anything that says Thursday because we are the Friday afternoon team the Good Friday team we are the team of suffering and death. He cries: What are we going to have for dinner? It is to avoid this question that the nun has her vocation. It's Friday and what can you expect? I'm bitter; I didn't want to die this young with my room in such a mess and with the authorities creeping in to take a look.

I wish we had the team again; but there is a secret government at work everywhere we look: in the leaves, in the wind. There is another secret team a secret against authority against any kind of prison. Yes, I'll pick you up at ten. If you play basketball for three hours, you can get rid of Jesus Christ Superstar. I know I would hate it; no one will go with the sad father who yearns for that movie. One thing is certain: it's Friday night because we got rid of Thursday forever.

The team is going backward like a train that roars down the aisle of forget-me-nots. Let's get together before I leave for Addis. He and his Addis and me and my revolutionary blue cheese meatloaf sandwich! There is no team and there never was. Your eyes will never close; there is no night, only blazing northern lights like illusory goals and citizens who need to be on fire with lies!

I am in Hell, in Florence. Forty-eight year old Sister Susannah Holy Hands puts on earrings and cries: He's looking at me! He's looking at me! I would much rather be with Friar Alberigo, a traitor to his friends and to his guests. I have fled to the bridge. In the snapshot I am alone on the Ponte Vecchio, the bridge between sanity and insanity, between being good and being bad. It must be November again; it must be Friday. The Guelphs and the Ghibellines run up to me.

I stand between a team that loses and a team that wins. Both teams are dressed in red. I can't decide which to join or is it my choice? The real danger comes to the victor, Aeschylus said. This happened so many centuries ago; how can I remember? Ten generations of poetry and Luke!

It rained for four days and four nights. I came to a deep black lake. There was no way back. I cried, Oh, my god! and sailed through in my small red ark. It was because I swore, because I prayed. I took with me two husbands two sons two daughters two cats two friends two teeth two clouds two forbidden Sundays two forbidden poems two forbidden victories two forbidden gods.

DEATHS AND ENTRANCES

My sons rise up and call me wicked
and burn me to death on the mountain
Here in the last moment of life I grow perfect
Here is peace experienced totally in one second

I look down on the skyscrapers of New York
I am luminous and tall, the tallest of them all, and far away

I am sitting on the edge of the bed on the edge of the earth
I am slipping   I am Moses I am Minervah the Impossible
Birds swoop down and feed me slogans

I run into a ruined church
A woman rises up points at a book and cries to me
Children of God   Children of God

I run out and buy a beautiful Easter egg
and give it to my daughter

Now I am on top of a mountain at night
close to a thousand stars   close to my children

To all homosexuals I send greetings
To all poets lovers and criminals greetings
I will not greet the saints
They are the only ones I will not recognize
Here on this mountain for a moment my own I am hospitable
I will send my love like a mountain stream down down to the depths

Come to the circus of mountains
We will leap through fiery hoops
We will be transfigured

TRAIN

I am on a train going to see my son
who vanished at fifteen

For distance: a waterfall
For immediacy: a gin and orange juice at noon

We got on at dawn and now it's twilight
The train takes a long time; perhaps forever

Lake Champlain must be the longest lake in the world
It has stopped and also the sun

We go to the dining car again
You look critically at me
like Peter Walsh looked at Clarissa Dalloway

The train is an hour late   the snow deeper

The sun has come back for a moment
in a long gold slice   Lake Champlain has turned up again
the density of these snow forests! mountains of
icicle-covered rocks bury me   There is nobody
out there nobody!   all of a sudden half the sky
becomes a passionate rose crying
Resurrection!   I don't want to get off this train

A WOMAN IN BLACK IN BOMBOOLA

Robert and I are living in Bomboola
It's very dangerous here; outside the hedge, bullets are flying
Robert! Robert! with his red personality
Bomboola is living inside us
Bomboola is crying: wife, wife
           why are you a wife?
Blood was spilled on my madonna gray silk dress
I didn't want to come to this reception in a manger
It is strange drinking bourbon
           while standing on straw
           next to a donkey
But Robert says that it's O.K. to be here
           that my Bomboolese is good
           and that I'm saying the right things.
"It must be rough on the road, the woods moan,"
           I say to an important cow.
The hours crawl
           It is such a long reception
Then I learn something new
Nuns have become prostitutes in Bomboola
Sister Maureen, the principal of the only Catholic girls' school
           in Bomboola has turned the school
           into a house of prostitution
I am shocked
I am not shocked
I ask if I may enter
           because all the bourbon and blood
           have ruined my gray madonna dress.

While making love to a lot of wild Bomboolans
           under the strict supervision of Sister Lily
I also try to write "A Short History of the Short Story"

but all I can remember is Chekhov and I,
Masha, in a black dress, sobbing
together down a long road
that can never lead to Moscow!
By this time Robert's personality has turned blue
he is beginning to weary of my wandering ways
He calls me a Jew and votes against me in the Assembly
Nobody understands my mercenary mousey personality
and all that it contains: an eraser
to wipe optimism from the earth
Maybe I should receive the Nobel Prize
But everyone in Sweden has forgotten me
except Mother
who is worried about all the daggers
that are aimed at me every night
in the nuns' prostitutes' house in Bomboola
It is tiring, Mother,
but it seems to be my vocation
here among the good sisters
where I am comparatively safe
(In the real Bomboola there is no such place, Robert moans.)

I am well aware of the importance of dying
My son, Paul Morel, will poison me to death in any case
It was foreseen by D.H. Lawrence long ago
Soon I will ask to be excused from this poem
But first I'd like to race up the hill to Selby
where the lights of the town are shining
Granddaddy Selby suddenly rises up
looking puritanical
and asks me about my marks
Marks! Marks! I've never had any marks, Granddaddy!
I am nothing
but the light of lights of Selby!
Robert rescues me from this delirium
and takes me to an island off the coast of Pusuka
(I have to misspell every place Robert goes so he won't be
assassinated!)

He says the most soothing thing:
            You are a nun
I know my fate at last
            and an eternal look creeps into my eye
            for a minute
But the river slides by in a body
            a soft body
Then Robert looks alarmed and cries: save me!
But a bomb falls on him
so I refuse

A gray deathly dawn creeps over the poem
The end of the poem, I gasp to my son
            there must be an end to the poem
It is New Year's Eve in the year 1999
I drink the poisoned cup of milk and honey
            that my son gives me
And laugh farewell
            at the twentieth century
            as I leap into my grave
            knowing that only a word has died
            and that I will become the resurrection and the life
                of all my sons. . .

This is the end
            of the crazy
                woman in black in Bomboola

PRELUDE FOR EPIPHANY

The icing on the wedding cake has melted.

Minerva, I don't care about your relationship
with Roberto! It is my relationship with Roberto that matters!
I am primary! You are secondary!
(I said these inane things
in a suburban French restaurant
while eating turbot with a thick sauce.)

My middle son, Jean, is trying to put the icing back
on the wedding cake.

François, my first born, I have a red spot
in my heart for you.
If only you wouldn't think black.
You are, alas, like your father

a man I admire very much
but would not care to imitate
but have imitated beyond belief.

Wittgenstein says to me:
Blindness is a dark picture in your soul.
Matisse says to me:
Your soul is an orange flower.
Picasso says to me:
You are a Judas. You disgust me.

It is impossible to put the icing back
on the wedding cake.

I want to do some traveling songs now.
About a wedding cake that keeps on going
on land, air and sea

The icing stays on
the bride and groom stay on

Roberto and I are one!

2

If I hadn't gone to graduate school
        and become a poet
        you boys would have had piano lessions.

My youngest son, Benny,
        thinks he was named after Benedict Arnold.
        That's why Benny is scared.

It's midnight.
Jean and Benny are fighting in the kitchen.
Tangerines are flying
Nana cannot sleep.
I go downstairs. I shout.
The boys laugh.

Chopin is waiting in the wings

in the black hallway
which is full of hiking boots.
Chopin will save the day
with a prelude
but Roberto is asleep.
So Chopin,
will you please come upstairs
and tell me about your life
which sounds interesting and strange?
However, the bed is half-full already!
also, the boys are upstairs and downstairs
at the same time.
Since I have failed them culturally,
I do not want to fail them morally as well, you understand!
The problem is, Chopin, we have no piano!

3

The next day, Epiphany.
Nana has just left.
Nana, who is afraid of cats.
Now the cats can come up from the cellar!
Enter Albert and Francette!
But the poor cats are frightened.

Football is on T. V. today.
Chopin, I forget which team — . I'm a poet — I haven't time —
as a girl I was delicate —
but my sons are very interested in blood sports.
Listen to their raucous laughter.
Look at the pot on that player!
He's past his prime: forty-eight, but still playing!
These linebackers are really something!
What a trio!

Josephine descends in her royal robes.
Josephine is my only daughter the queen.
She wants to take dancing lessons
at the Murray Louis Dance Company
but I haven't any money.
I can't interest her in blood sports.
Josephine is tempestuous and flies from the living room.

Chopin coughs up blood.
I offer him some Beaujolais but there are bits of cork in it.
Then I offer him diet ginger ale
but he is afraid to take it.
I have forgotten all my French.
Chopin has forgotten all his English.
So we tell a few Polish jokes together
or rather I translate into Polish
from Benny's ethnic joke book
which Roberto has hidden
in the linen closet.

Finally, I come up from the cellar
with a piano for Chopin and I heave it into the kitchen!
Chopin fumbles a bit at first.

The first prelude is beautiful but too short.
I ask if he would please lengthen it.
He will work on it, he promises.
The second prelude is full of Bartok-like dissonances.
It hate, it. I long for beauty and this is ugly.
Chopin apologizes, coughs up blood.
Chopin points out that the next prelude will be played
at his funeral. I feel as if I were there.
But I am here and Chopin is dying in my house!
I give him a clean handkerchief
so that there'll be no blood on the keys.

The afternoon is passing, soon the light will be gone
and the Wise Men will have gone back to the East, empty-handed.

There are gutteral sounds from the other room:
Mom, when are we gonna hit the road
and go to the deli for beer? François says.
You aren't going to the deli for beer, Roberto says.
Everyone is going to help me take down the Christmas tree;
we'll play Christmas carols!
Are you kidding? says François, who is mad about the beer.
(Please, Mom, beer.
It sounds like a prayer.)

Tomorrow François leaves for a bohemian hideaway
in the far north, the mountains.
Nana has flown back to her Victorian Catholic world
in the Deep South.

Now Chopin is playing a subterranean prelude.
The prelude grows louder and louder.
The boys begin to complain about Chopin.
Chopin is in hell, I explain.
I say that this is the dream of my life come true:
to be in hell with Chopin.
Roberto looks hurt. But goes on reading *The Times*.

Epiphany is almost over.
The Wise Men have arrived just in time to save us!
But they say that they can only stay a minute.

Strange things are going on in our house; don't leave! I beg them.
(Benny is planning to run away; the Wise Men might have an idea.)
But the Wise Men explain that to stay

would be to act without precedent.
Tradition demands
that they depart by sundown.
So I walk with the Wise Men to the end of the driveway.

I grew up in Great Neck, which is in the East, I say.
No, say the Wise Men, Great Neck is West.
I go back to the house, which is now empty.

The telephone rings.
It is my little sister, Anna.
I've shot the sea gull! she cries.
You shouldn't have done that, Anna.
Then I become confused.
I thought she was the sea gull.
But Anna has hung up.

Roberto will never return.
François, Jean and Benny will never return.
Nana, Josephine and the cats will never return.

The Wise Men have vanished forever with the sun.
Chopin is still alive, of course, but where?

THE MOCKINGBIRD

to my mother

Hello, New Orleans!
city of my birth and death!

This is going to be the strangest visit
I've ever had to New Orleans
because there's something the matter with me
Don't stop listening! I won't talk about it!
As long as someone is listening I'm alive
That's my oleander tree blossoming outside my window
Two years ago it was just beginning to turn white
and now it's all white.
Strange to be walking through mother's house.
All the photographs of the dead!
My father, grandfather, greatgrandmother
I'm sitting in a tub full of scalding water —
Why? Because I like to —
If all the great writers in the world hang up on me,
will I call back and promise to
do what makes sense to them?
Emily, I wish you were here. . .
Sit on the pale blue taffeta dressing table chair of my mother's
Don't faint. I'll pull the shower curtain shut.

Yesterday was Easter.
Lonely Easter dinner. Just the three of us.
Vivaldi, Mary Magdalene, Jimmy.
Well, we deserve it.
How long do I have to stay in this tub?
Please don't tell me!
Emily doesn't know.
I'm dying
to find out

but I can't see
Greak Neck 2073
that's an ancient phone number
If you try it, you'll get Sparta
It was rather peculiar being a Spartan girl if you remember
The boys were trained to be soldiers
and the girls were given piano lessons
I'm going to have to investigate this dichotomy
My memory is failing soon I'll be blind and mute
Don't kid about it it could happen
My oleander tree
my dogwood tree
my dog snapped at the ankles
of my gentlemen callers
if I were by Tennessee Williams
which in a way I am because mother is
I'm really a Chekhov woman because I don't do enough about my "situation"
I've let my talent rot in a gothic school
in a gothic suburb in a gothic family
I'm supposed to be the mother of

Emily, don't leave! Have a cup of tea!
Please play the piano in case you're bored.
Vinnie will be down in a minute!

I am not a martyr. I don't wear a cross between my eyes.
I want life, love and deliverance from evil
To Hell with Simone Weil!
I want to keep my round hazel eyes opened forever!

My dog snapped at my future husband's ankles
every time he visited me
I was a bride in Paris
People envy you   you envy yourself
and wonder why you're lonely
Do you remember the Paris apartment we sublet in desperation one summer?
The decor was entirely Chinese
I tried not to be nervous but I didn't belong there

so I spent the morning in a corner of the dining room
the least Chinese room playing the recorder
or in the bathroom washing out all my sweaters in Woolite
        imported from home
Then I'd run into the Chinese living room
and put the sweaters on towels on the Chinese lacquered tables
and run out   I'd go downstairs
and ask the ferocious concierge
if I had any mail, which I did, a gentle letter from my father
telling me that my dog was dead
so I ran out into the hot empty gray rue de Turin
(all the street names in that quarter were Arabic)
all shutters closed nobody alive but me!

Do you have any more travel stories to tell
No I don't

My oleander tree
if I could find my glasses I could see it
Found them!
So I can describe the blossom
Each blossom is composed of five circular white petals.
The tree is covered with thousands of them and is two stories tall.
Thank you for describing *your* oleander tree so well!

I want very much to go to the cemetery
then if we have time and I feel like it
and you do we can go to the art museum
some big Egyptian thing is going on there
I'm not too hot for Egyptian things
Too many young girls
buried alive beside their fathers

Mother cut the first magnolia blossom off a tree
and put it in a vase
It smells like lemon and looks like wax
gigantic, white, an ugly bride

Emily, would you leave home, like Nora
and have affairs with Tolstoy, Chekhov, Ibsen, Virginia Woolf
—somebody!
at your age at my age
I don't want sex with anybody!
I've got something the matter. . .
I could go on but will eat ice cream instead.

If we went to the cemetery tonight
we would have to make reservations
or stand around outside waiting
to be saved to be saddened
I can't stand around too long
My father may not know I am here
and I've got to go on writing
I'm very ambitious mother is saying about me
Neruda said that any serious poet
who says he/she isn't vain is a liar.
Neruda got depressed when someone, by accident, praised Lorca.

Do you mind going to Mass?
No, I don't mind going to Mass on Tuesday.
Does my mother think I am an atheist?
The truth about Aunt Margaret is
she would never miss her sewing circle every Wednesday
She is a talented artist
but her works are perfect copies.
Witty Aunt Eva is dying prematurely of a brain disease.
At the end of Ibsen's "Ghosts"
with the snow dancing the tarantella
outside the log cabin
I sit watching in horror
as Oswald, dying of a brain disease,
leaps through the window
like my dream of a lion in the snow
heading toward the sun.

The New Orleans air smells so sweet and light

I could lift it without worrying!
Mother is calling, "Come see the magnolia
It's gotten ten times larger!"
I take one look and step back.
Mother says I seem afraid of it.
Who else in the world would be afraid of a magnolia!

Are you free?
Are you free on Friday?
The French Quarter looks as free as ever
but there's a murderer running loose in all the courtyards
Mother and Aunt Margaret in blue silk
and I in a green Israeli army uniform
In the Courtyard of the Two Sisters and the Niece/Daughter
we sit and rest and watch the fountain.
We are history!
But there's nothing in it except big goldfish.

I hear a mockingbird
I hear a phone call from a doctor
The crazy magnolia blossom has turned brown turned senile
I'm no longer afraid of it
I tell the doctor I am being fairly active
Sexually? he asks.
No, I'm visiting my mother.
Urologists are just as funny as psychiatrists
The magnolia looks innocent
as long as it stays on the tree
if you pick it it becomes the mad dog
that bit me on Holy Thursday.

I lay awake last night thinking of my students
I had a whole scene going strong, very strong
The Principal and I, Josephine and her mother
If Josephine fails English senior year. . .
A Chinese torture chamber opens its doors
I push in Josephine
Why shouldn't she be tortured

she's done nothing wrong.
Many students just don't care.
Even T.S. Eliot thought this a legitimate spiritual problem
I have no desire to quarrel with him
I have no desire. . .
A doctor calls and says something meaningless
Am I a unique statistic
now that spring is here
How many songs can one mockingbird sing
Mother says seventeen
There's another virginal magnolia blossom on the tree

PARALLELOGRAM

If the plane doesn't crash
I'll be 49 tomorrow.
Plane crashes
UNKNOWN POET ON BOARD FATAL FLIGHT

49 planes
carrying one unknown poet crash.
The 49 parts of the poet's
flying imagination become known.

The birthday occurs
in the Serpentine.

The poet likes to travel
through life
but suffers from the same disturbances
as Mahatma Ghandi.
These disturbances
are constitutional.

While wandering through
St. James Park
in desperation
the poet found a toilet
For Children Under Eleven only.
As the poet continued
a man in a blue coat
with "Cake House" stitched on it
signaled her.
A ladies' toilet, he called
is farther down
across the bridge!

This disturbed the poet.
since she hadn't inquired.
The expression on her face
must have been strange.

The same expression
was on the face
of Mahatma Ghandi.

Also, on the face
of Charles the First
while he was marched
through St. James Park
to be beheaded.

The poet buys a banana
in Trafalgar Square
where a thousand people are.
Runs into the National Portrait Gallery
sits down on the guard's chair.
It's quiet in here.
Dizzy again. Good god!
Look at Queen Anne!
All of her seventeen
children died young.
And then she assumed the throne!
I would have assumed nothing.

Lady Mary Selby
was a literary blue stocking
in London in the 18th century.
Were there ever any male blue stockings?
I hate that term
but I like to think about Lady Mary.

James Barry, an Irish painter.
was forthright and quarrelsome.
Is it all right to behave that way then?

There are 500 poets
on this jumbo jet.
All have yellow roses
across their female breasts
which do not keep
the wings from collapsing.
On the contrary, they are intimidating!

Alexander Pope
was a formidable poet
with a large circle
of enemies and friends
Sounds more like a parallelogram.

Shakespeare at 46
6 years before his death.
A romantic genius
with a balding dome.
No sign of greatness;
just an earring
and an amused light.

Keats is with Shakespeare!
If he had known—
he did.
Keats' portrait by Severn the smallest
but of his whole self.
No malice or madness
in him yet.
Lucky Keats
he didn't live long enough!

Ambulance siren zooms through London
to take care of all problems.
How like civilization!
To keep on reading about Rhodesia
in The Times.

In the Blake Room at the Tate
The Self-Murderers are owls.
I thought owls were wise.

The Morning After the Deluge
is more than we can bear
so we don't
it bears us away.
"Away" is an interesting word
since we're still here.
Maybe it means we
don't care much so long
as the scenes change.

Ambulance siren again.
Ambulance contains
the long lost Septimus Smith
by Virginia Woolf.
No doctor
egotist or altruist
could have stopped
Septimus
just as some years later
no one could stop his creator.

I brought my mother and daughter
to London! What a noble idea!
After two weeks I'm broke.
How relieved I am to sign away
my last traveller's check
the last cent I possess!
Mother is amazed at my determination!
I, who only three weeks ago, proclaimed
Money is freedom!

"She is like this
in real life too."

I was born in the year '28
the year before the crash
I couldn't be a Catholic poet
too much turbulence in the sky in my head
I've unfastened my seat belt
The plane's movie screen flashes white
FATAL POET CRASHES INTO
INNOCENT DAUGHTER
Poet Innocent Too

Hello!
I'm an American poet
of the twentieth century.
My dates are 1964–1977.
That's a short life.
I know. I got a late start.
And am always killing myself off.
I was lucky to be a poet at all.
You can't paint my portrait.
I'm too white.
But I've got a daughter
very talented, pretty and nineteen.
In her flowered London dress before
my shadow withers the flowers—
paint her!

The Plane's Wing enters Cinderella's mouth stretching it until she screams British Caledonia! so the Wing goes around the corner to Buckingham Palace but there are six corners twelve palaces and an infinite blackened wall so the Wing gives up and Beatrice calls to Dante from a car asks if he is lost he says yes she drives him to Grosvenor Gardens and says, Around the corner you'll find the satanic Wing of the Plane that smites Job but Dante says No! Satan must be stopped at Victoria Station a red bus with Satan on it is flying to Trafalgar Square to buy a banana to put in Job's mouth. He deserves it but cannot find the banana because people and pigeons take up every inch so Trafalgar himself sensing the difficulties of foreigners during the Jubilee summer leaps from his column finds a banana puts it in Job's mouth so Satan's conscience is clearing

up the sky full of pigeons disappears the Plane's Wing goes ripping back to an androgynous novelist Woolf sitting in Russell Square Park she has never met Dante has wanted to so gives him a cigar and a yellow rose. Virginia is full of yellow roses which are androgynous so the Plane's Wing kisses all of them thus being late for her final appointment with a psychiatrist who is in love with her so the doctor hides behind coffee specs and a brown desk until The Wing in a gesture of generosity leaps over the desk for farewell kiss then twirls downstairs disappears into the East River knowing he must bring three lost Cinderellas to London that night. They need only one Wing to transform them into the Golden Girls of Grosvenor Gardens where Peter Walsh is waiting with his opened pocket knife to cut out their hearts and brains, the poor Cinderellas all of them Indian princesses fallen into low estate and Miss Kilman presides over the crucifixion of the race in her rain coat which is ugly

You cannot ever say that Woolf was a feminist novelist because Miss Kilman is so hideous. Then in comes Elizabeth in a pink dress. Clarissa Dalloway is an unsuccesful mother so Cinderella Girl rips the pink dress off Elizabeth gives it to Plane's Wing who runs to the Nun clutching a rosary and says, Here, have it. The Nun doesn't raise her eyes Dante stands before her pleading he has come so far forward for a two-week trip to London from the 14th century but the Nun's teeth are silver bullets. That scares Dante

The question of whether Mum Cinderella should live or die, succeed or fail is not resolved either so Cinderella Girl asks Dante for a safety pin because her pants are falling down and he cannot refuse a lovely young girl in stasis in the lobby of a changing world. Beatrice in modern dress is trying to escape from Dante who has suddenly assumed Byronesque proportions in Westminster Abbey. Step on Byron! Step on him, Annabelle, step on him! Step on T.S. Eliot! Stamp on him and forget him! Teach me to die and not to die teach me to stink well! I am the Hyacinth Girl but Dante snarls that the Hyacinth Girl is a churl. Put out the light! T.S. Eliot is dead! Put out the cat! T.S. Eliot is rising! The speechless guards who are there to protest and protect the bodies that rise had been told Satan was dead and did not recognize the Plane's Wing that tipped each guardsman with a gold coin that meant instant suicide in the Serpentine so Byron wakened by the fuss of Eliot in the next tomb tells him to shut up gets up himself and says what do you want? He knows damn well what Eliot wants but Byron has been dead so long his Armenian costume is in shreds so he decides to look for his sister but the Nun says he can't. Still she is having a mystical marriage with a Jesuit so she can't talk. And she secretly understands Byron's probing into the infinite sister

sitting on the bed late at night in Surrey and shouting, Screw your courage to the sticking place and we'll not fail! And that's just what happens. Byron fails. Mum Cinderella comes into the room unexpectedly and shouts, No potsmoking in this house, Get out! Byron slinks back to the Abbey.

In the meantime, Jimmy the Prince is chanting Room 42 Room 42 but the truth is there is no room 42 anywhere in the world and Jimmy is destined for Bus 24 because the Plane's Wing is too busy saving Satan, Job and Dante and giving everybody androgynous cigars. The hours are pouring off the neck of Big Ben and the days of the Cinderellas' visit are squeezed, shrunk, bitten, chewed and swallowed and the Plane's Wing is triumphant since he secretly desires the destruction of everybody! He desires nothing more than to Kilwoman so Mum Cinderella arrives in total trust and obedience in a gold raincoat, weird gleam in eye with Shakespeare's earring protruding from navel. Wing presses her keys and cries: This is the woman to kill! He knows how to do it having drowned her once in the East River already. She opens her mouth to scream but Wing maneuvers in rapidly giving her a chill because the Wing is icy then a thrill and she becomes thirsty for more but the yacht is approaching the coast and will not turn back

THE SLEEPING PRODIGAL

I have a daughter
Her name is Russia
My daughter is in Siberia
Russia, is our Soviet rule unreasonable
Are you O.K., my old companion

I am walking on a wooden bridge
Winters are severe in Leningrad
I'd better walk on a cast-iron bridge

Russia, my daughter of the auburn hair
defiant on the horizon at six p.m.
Russia, are you hiding in a black Maine woods
Autumnal twenty-year-old
Golden rod is a fragile wand

"Daughter" is a difficult word to type
When I leave out the t's
it's pale as dough
Am I walking against the light

Russia, I'll find you in one ikon or another
in Tschaikovsky's house at Klin
All that was holy I denied
I'll find you in Samarkand
in an open synagogue hidden
An old Islamic Jewish woman in swaddling clothes
sits next to me on a bench outside
She holds up nine fingers for nine children
I hold up four

Russia, put down your cross
The charioteer rushes across the sky
I'll find you in the mediaeval town of Suzdal
riding home on your bike at 5 p.m.
You are carrying a bouquet of red "Kan" flowers
I see your face your amber eyes amber hair hear your voice as clearly
as if this were the real world and not a museum
the 20th century and not the 13th
How familiar it is to find you in a foreign country
among warm babies in carriages in red knit caps
being pushed by self-forgetful young mothers
chilly in summer flowered dresses!
To be lost in Suzdal!
to sit here watching everyone go home to dinner
I wave you on, czarina

Russia, the red sky is falling but don't worry
Tamerlane's tomb will take its place
Take your places, everybody
Sons and daughters, take your places
Put your napkins in your laps
In Tamerlane's tomb chew with your mouths closed
Don't be sorry   A taxi is coming
to take us to the Moscow bomb shelter
Chew your food slowly
If you are ever a guest in someone's house in Stalingrad
Hold your fork this way
The driver is your older brother
The taxi his old blue truck
Russia, believe in God and in sanity under these circumstances
Even I could not have dreamed up my strange personality
or the four heartbeats inside my womb moving onward
Am I the wonder of refinement
leading my children into Mongolian captivity
There must be a Russian god that allows this
Take your wooden chalice   please hand it to us all   we are waiting

ODE

in memory of Mother Assumpta

O, normal cloud, so pleased to be in that great sky
O, even-tempered bus, plodding on a certain route
O, simple lake, unpuzzled by the sun
    That altruistic sky never neglects anyone
    To be a posthumous letter that could reach
    to be a thing
    That orange truck never procrastinates
    The Massachusetts Turnpike has no regrets
    If I were to become the whole northeastern section
    of the United States
    That would be an achievement of innocence

    Follow your conscience
    at a safe distance
    There was to have been no funeral   I didn't attend
    There is no guilt in golden rod
    nor sorrow in the forests of Maine
    That cloud inside my head is locked
    I did not respond

    Still, these pine trees
        these estranged daughters
            lean against each other
                wait

WAITING FOR GOD THAT COWARD

I am taking
my almost rejected dream
into the city —

yellow shirts
were hanging
on the chain
of the storm door
parallel to the sun

I carried
those cowards
into the dark
house   I wanted to
lie down and die
of course

But the dream
held me tight
in a panic
I unhooked my bra
unbuttoned my skirt
and lay down
waiting for God
In three minutes
he said, Get up

So I got dressed
picked up *The Times*
threw it down
kicked it —

It's nuts doing it now
I can't abort
a storm
My house
is a falsely lit wood

and that nightmare
last night
being in a grounded plane
but still moving
seeing my silver skeleton
armbones neatly folded
lying on the runway

This is Thursday afternoon
under the river

go up to the university
lift this plane into the air
you're doing it now

BLUE PAJAMAS

I am very sorry to have to tell you about Joe
        although I hardly remember him
                You say I spoke to him on the phone in October
                        when he was trying vainly to reach you

I don't want to believe he was such a good friend of yours
        He was selling drugs in Harlem when he was murdered
                His body was found in the Bronx on Thanksgiving
                        He could have been my son
                                if we hadn't sent you away to the mountains

I wonder if I feel superior to his mother
        with whom I have so much in common
                I met her in Gordon's Men's Shop where she works
                        We looked fearfully at each other
                                although we spoke about blue pajamas
                                        which she wrapped carefully as a gift

HALLOWEEN IN LEMONGRAD

You are ordered to appear at the Lemongrad Academy on Halloween at 9 p.m. Your son, Benny Light on the Mayonovsky, is the subject of a Soviet Communique, of which the principle word is 'diktat.'

Benny's mother, Almondina Amandorova, tries to believe in God and in all of the other persons who have hindered her career. When Premier Joseph Stolen, dictator of the Lemongrad Academy, hears about Almondina poems, full of creeping cupolas, he is incensed. Almondina admits that she was once a Christian criminal but that she now believes in Joe. The death of Joseph Stolen is imminent, but, since he doesn't know it, he gives Almondina a long, boring lecture on her fuzzy attitude. If she continues to write absurd fantasies, her child will be doomed. Almondina becomes frantic. She distracts herself by observing the lighted pumpkin in the window of Joe Stolen's study. The light of the world has been reduced to this! She continues to maintain a silent, gothic facade. She observes some totally black paintings that are not unusual. They turn out to be widows in Joe's study, which is a converted tomb.

Benny Light on the Mayonovsky sets fire to the Academy. He is immediately expelled. The reason for Benny's deed is paradoxical: one of the black paintings is of Dostoevsky, full of inspired serenity in Cell #9. But this painting reminds Benny of all the painful years he spent stuffed in the Orange Chimney for punishment. When the Lemongrad Academy has burned down completely, Benny still isn't sorry. Premier Stolen screams prophetically that Benny will be inside the fiery pumpkin before the night is over. Hearing this, Almondina becomes hysterical and flies out of the ruins. Bennetchka scrambles after her. Gugl, husband and father, slumps into the Chair of Despair. Premier Joe screams at him, "You see what you've got?" Benny whispers to the collapsed Almondina that this is the scariest Halloween in his colorful, short life.

It is true that prospects do not seem bright for Benny Light on the Mayonovsky and his ashen parents. So, for a change of pace, they walk briskly to Nevsky Prospekt and hop on the Nevsky Trolley. It is an ill-starred trolley, Zhivago explains to them later in the Cemetery. (Sorry for skipping ahead.) Through the trolley window, Almondina sees an old woman in an orange dress, walking parallel to the trolley. Almondina realizes that the old woman is a parallelism so she pushes Benny and Gugl off the trolley just in time. One minute later, the old woman falls dead on the sidewalk. The little nuclear family glances at the unfamiliar corpse and marches on.

Naturally, Benny is concerned about his future at the Lemongrad Academy. He decides to go back to the ruins and face Comrade Joe. Benny knows that part of the punishment for his latest crime will involve standing in the freezing Pool of Turtles for months, possibly forever. Everyone in the Eastern world, who has shown disrespect for Joe, will be punished in the same way. So the Pool of Turtles will have to be enlarged. The lines of world-wide Bennys reach over all the bridges of Lemongrad, until there are no bridges left, only drowning Bennys. Almondina has the Brooklyn Bridge flown over so that the excess of Bennys will not have to spend the night in the Neva. This is a secret gesture of good will and goodnight because everyone is wet and exhausted. It is Mom Almondina's and Benny's secret, since there are too many dissidents and not enough dictators, as always, love, Mom.

Due to worry, Almondina and Gugl have simultaneous heart attacks, which reunite them as man and wife. The immediate cause is their 11:30 p.m. visit with Zhivago in the Cemetery for Lemongraduates. From the air above the Cemetery, Lemongrad looks a lot like Newark. Millions of green lights that seem to be those of any eternal city are just grapes. This is the last humiliation and agony that the tormented couple has to endure at the hands of Premier Joe. If Joe will let them be destroyed by heart attacks and by the Benny Problem, as it has come to be known in the Eastern world, he will also not rest until Newark is destroyed. Everyone in the world confirms this judgment. The Western world joins the Eastern world in apostasy. Nobody believes in Joe S. anymore.

There is something still bothering the star-shaped ego of Almondina. If Lemongrad and Newark were to merge, thus solving the world problem of illusionary grapes, the Karenin Award for Criminal Greatness would still go to President Buddy's slavish advisor, Lemonode. Lemonode will win, not through genius, but through nepotism and corny hypocrisy.

Halloween is almost over. Joseph Stolen accidentally discovers that he is going to commit suicide in a few minutes. He becomes subdued and eats nothing except a few peanuts in preparation for the event.

Almondina is wearing a new martyred smile, for which Gugl will have to pay. However, he is preoccupied with singing a new rendition of "Home, Home on the Stove." Gugl does not belong on the stove. Almondina doesn't think that she does. If this is her fuzzy attitude, why should anyone care that Almondina will never again receive the Karenin Award for Criminal Greatness?

As midnight strikes, the Poetess and the Potboiler look up to see their son Bennetchka saunter into the ruined Academy. Laughing, he lights a match to the fading pumpkin. Then Benny throws the pumpkin, containing Premier Joe, into the Fontanka. Its radiant fury can be seen throughout a hastily reunited world. All Saints Day can begin to dawn.

Dawn received zero on the final exam.
That was original.
So, I pretended she wasn't there.
Original, too.
She wrote wonderful things
About the honesty of Willy Loman.
So I gave her a star
For being present instead of past.
She wrote a good poem before she went nuts.
And this must be recorded
Before I, too, descend onto the tracks.
They've rebuilt the tracks
And the rocky cliff.
They've rebuilt the sunlight
Made it more intense
Rebuilt the lost navy blue dress
As I move toward ugliness
A seductive fact.

DOUBLE VISION

Epicurus: Wisdom is the highest pleasure
             and Sorrow is an evil.

Father Ted: That's wrong.
             Sorrow is not an evil.

Epicurus: Sorrow endured for a long time
             can lead to a higher pleasure

Eloise: You're both wrong!

             Here is Sorrow!
                 A young girl
                 dressed in purple and lavender
                 sitting on a bench
                 in the Musée du Luxembourg
                 reading a little gold book.

             Here is Pleasure!
                 An old hag
                 dressed in black rage
                 crawling in the back door of the villa
                 to eat garbage.

             Pleasure, go spend the night with Father Ted.
             Sorrow, come home with me and be my child.

THE DEPARTURE OF FLORIMELL
for Lita Hornick

She ran out of Time and onto the Half-moon
Who swung her to a blindfolded field.
She ran out of Time and into Cowardice
Who stitched her a mourning veil of yellow leaves.
She ran out of Time and into Fear
Who kissed her with bullets of protection.
She ran out of Time and into a wall
Where she vanished in the last glisten of a stone.

She ran out of Time to the grave of her father
Who didn't recognize her any longer.
She ran out of Time and into the woods
Where crickets rang for Night and the Dragon.
She ran out of Time and into Poverty
Where she refused the bloody handkerchief of Saint Thérèse
Where Winter arrived in a freakish Storm
And tossed her Villon's watery scarf.

She ran out of Time and into the Church
Where a cruel fisherman chanted the Magnificat.
She ran out of Time and into a pearl
Where she heard two planes collide and catch fire
And crash into the criss-crossed arms of her shell.

She ran out of Time and into a slain violin
From which she transfigured the adulterous man
Into a white horse on the wandering heath of King Lear.
She could see the abandoned pillar
From under Zimbabwe's willow tree.
She watered the Sahara with Christmas lights
And sang "God Save Queen Mab" to the compassionate witch.

She invited all priests and politicians to come to a cloud
Where she served them the Soup of Faith
Made of tyrants' bones. This she did in good faith
Faith as clear as twenty-year-old skin.
She ran out of Time and into Merlin
Whose face was of ebony whose red robe was Satan's.
In his mirror she saw her own blindness for the next pall.
She heard her son crying in a well
And embraced his mocking shadow on her path.
She ran out of Time. Chrysanthemums sprang
From fireflies in the Garden of Prometheus.